The Termite-r

by Tom McLaughlin
Illustrated by Bill Ledger

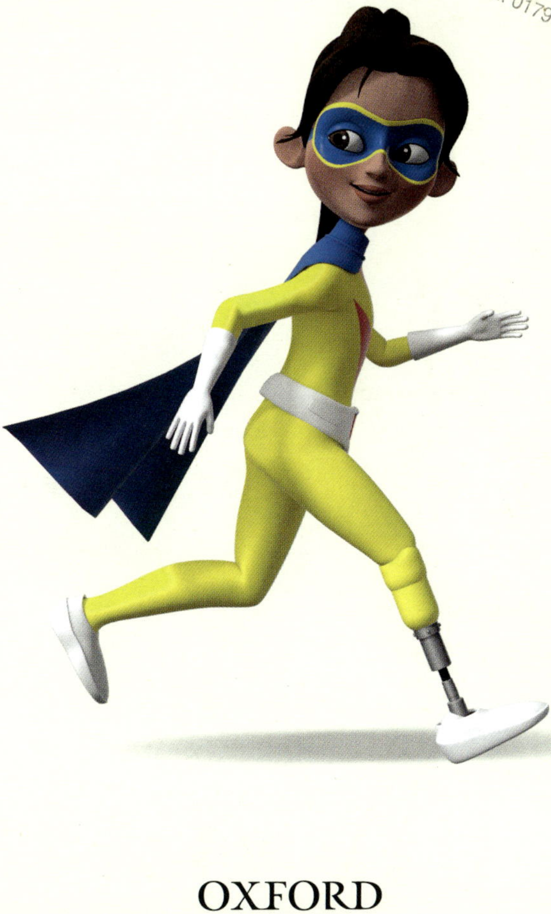

OXFORD
UNIVERSITY PRESS

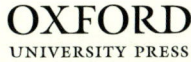

In this story ...

Evan
(Flex)

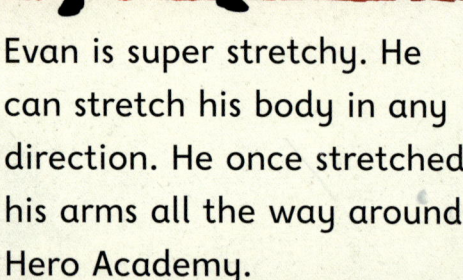

Evan is super stretchy. He can stretch his body in any direction. He once stretched his arms all the way around Hero Academy.

Nisha
(Nimbus)

Nisha has the power to control the weather. She can make it sunny or stormy. Once she stopped some baddies by trapping them in a tornado.

Chapter 1:
Evan's dilemma

Evan was struggling to make a decision. It was the most important decision of his day.

"I just don't know, Nisha. Should I go for raspberry or strawberry?" he asked, scratching his head and staring at the two jars of jam in front of him.

Suddenly, there was a loud rumble. Evan looked up, surprised.

"You'd better decide quickly," Nisha said, through a mouthful of toast. "I can hear your belly growling from here."

"That's not me!" Evan cried out, as the dinner hall wobbled like a jelly. "It's coming from outside!"

Just then, a shrill *BRIIIIIING!* filled the air. Alarms all over the school started ringing.

"It's a red alert!" shouted Nisha, clinging on to the table as the room shook again.

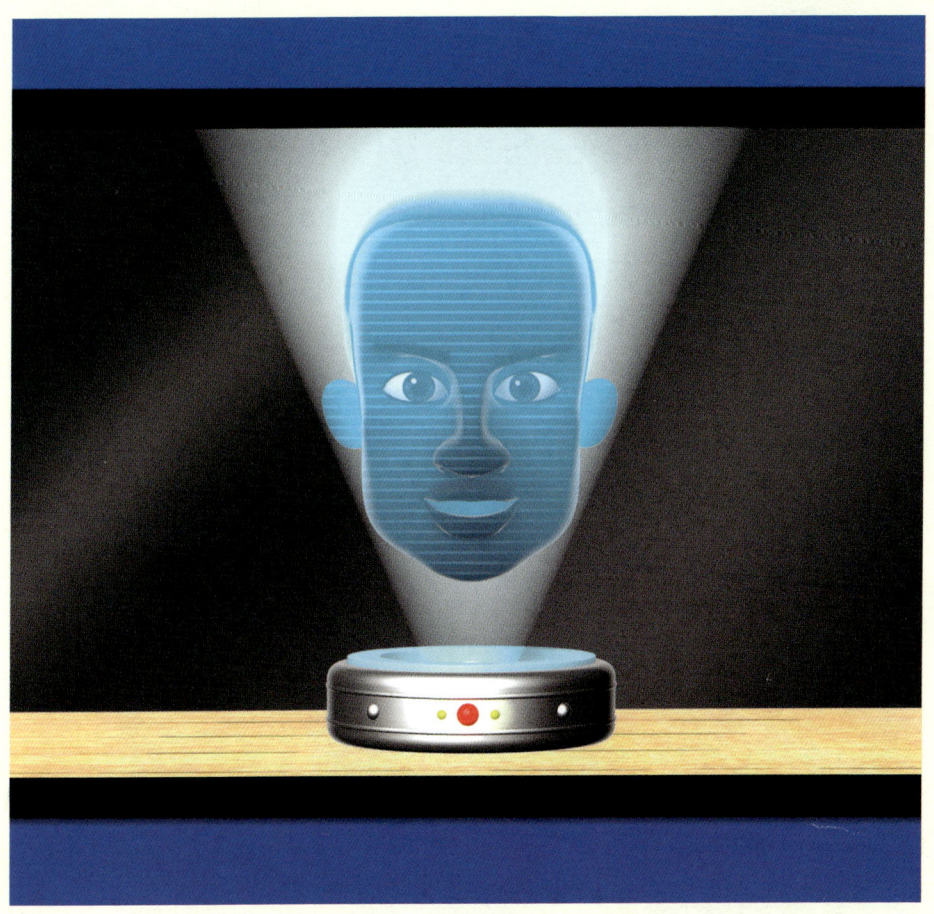

Suddenly, the Head appeared on a screen in the dinner hall. "This is a BIG emergency. Lexis City is under attack from a mystery creature!" he said, in alarm. "Nisha, Evan ... I need you two to investigate at once. There's no time to lose!"

"We're on our way," Evan said.

"You can count on us," added Nisha.

Nisha and Evan quickly spun into their super suits, becoming Nimbus and Flex. Then they dashed to the door.

"Wait!" the Head called after them.

"Sir?" Flex said, skidding to a stop.

"If it was up to me," replied the Head with a grin, "I'd go for strawberry every time."

Chapter 2:
Robot alert!

Nimbus and Flex raced through the streets of Lexis City, following the rumbling noise.

"We're heading towards Police Commissioner Jordan's office!" Flex yelled above the noise, which was getting louder and louder.

They turned a corner and came to a sudden halt. A gigantic robot loomed in front of them.

Nimbus's mouth dropped open in shock.

"It looks like a giant insect!" Flex said, unable to take his eyes off the metal monster.

"I AM THE TERMITE-NATOR!" the robot bellowed. Its metallic voice echoed off the buildings. "OUT OF MY WAY, TINY HUMANS!" It opened its jaws like a hungry rubbish truck and took a huge bite out of Police Commissioner Jordan's office. Bits of brick and plaster fell out of its giant mouth and landed on the street below.

"I thought *I* was a messy eater!" yelled Flex, diving for cover behind a tree.

Nimbus ducked down next to him. "This is a disaster! I hope Commissioner Jordan is all right."

"Uh oh!" Flex exclaimed. "Looks like the Termite-nator is going back for a second helping!"

Chapter 3:
See you later, Termite-nator

The heroes watched in horror as the Termite-nator took another enormous bite out of Police Commissioner Jordan's office. The whole wall had now been chomped off. They could see the commissioner inside, glaring at the Termite-nator. She was holding her two terrified dogs, Tick and Tock.

"How dare you!" Commissioner Jordan shouted at the gigantic robot. "You can devour as much of my office as you want, but I will not stand for *anyone* upsetting my dogs."

"We've got to do something!" Flex said to Nimbus.

Just then, the Termite-nator reached out with a huge metal grabber and scooped the commissioner and her dogs into the air. The dogs yapped furiously, but the Termite-nator ignored them.

There was a grinding noise as the robot's belly opened.

"It's got a cage in there!" Nimbus cried.

The robot put the commissioner and her dogs inside the cage.

"I've got a plan!" Flex said. He held on to the tree that they were hiding behind with one arm. With his other arm, he stretched across the street and grabbed on to a lamp-post, so that it was stretched like a trip wire.

"Good idea!" exclaimed Nimbus. "I'll get its attention." She ran towards the Termite-nator and waved her arms. "Hey, you big pile of junk!" she yelled.

The robotic beast turned towards the heroes.

"Bet you can't catch me," Nimbus shouted, racing back towards the tree and hurdling over Flex's arm.

The Termite-nator stepped effortlessly over Flex. "HA, HA! YOU CAN'T STOP ME THAT EASILY!" it bellowed. Then it reached down and yanked up the tree that Flex was wrapped round and threw it on the ground.

Flex snapped back to his normal shape and got away just in time.

"Let me try," Nimbus said to Flex. She summoned up a powerful gust of wind, blowing it towards the Termite-nator. The robot wobbled, stumbled backwards, then – with an almighty *CRASH!* – landed in a heap on the ground.

The door to the cage sprang open as the Termite-nator hit the street.

Nimbus and Flex clambered over the rubble to help the commissioner out of the cage.

"Are you OK?" Flex asked the commissioner.

"I'm all right," she replied. "The dogs are a bit shaken up, but they'll be fine … thanks to you."

Flex breathed a sigh of relief. He smiled at Nimbus. "Job well done!" he said.

Then the Termite-nator began to move again.

Chapter 4: Doctor Bug

"Look! Something's happening to the robot!" Flex said, pointing at the wreckage of the Termite-nator.

Nimbus and the commissioner turned and saw a hatch opening at the top of the Termite-nator's head. Slowly, one hand appeared, then another ... and another!

A tiny man emerged from the hatch. He was wearing a suit of armour that made him look just like a termite. The antennae on his helmet wiggled as he moved. Nimbus and Flex tried not to giggle.

"Nobody move!" shouted the insect man. "Fear the mighty Doctor Bug! I built the Termite-nator to destroy you all! I imagine that I'll be shooting straight to the top of your Most Wanted Villains list, won't I, Commissioner?"

Police Commissioner Jordan snorted with laughter. "You? Number one on the Most Wanted Villains list? Hardly."

"And why not?" Doctor Bug demanded.

"Erm ... I think Ray Ranter is number one," Nimbus said.

"Silence!" shrieked the tiny man.

"Did you do all this just because you wanted to be top of my Most Wanted Villains list?" the commissioner asked, raising her eyebrows.

"Yes. I mean, no. I mean ... maybe." He shuffled his feet. "So what number am I on the list? Two?" Doctor Bug asked hopefully.

"More like twenty-two," the commissioner scoffed.

"WHAT?" Doctor Bug folded his arms furiously. "I *will* make it to the top of that list. You'll see."

"Not if you're in jail," said Flex, stretching out an arm to grab him.

The tiny villain dodged out of Flex's way and jumped high in the air. Wings appeared from the back of his insect suit, and he whizzed away before Flex could reach him.

Doctor Bug

NUMBER 22 MOST WANTED VILLAIN

Catchphrase: Tremble before me, puny humans!

Hobby: going on safari in Wildcroft Woods to spot rare insects.

Likes: pollen squash, honey cake.

Dislikes: magnifying glasses, Venus flytraps.

Beware! This villain may be small but he has armies of robotic insects under his control – so always carry a fly-swatter, just in case!

Actual size (cm)

Chapter 5:
Invasion!

Back at Hero Academy, Evan and Nisha walked into the dinner hall.

"Where is everyone?" Evan said.

"There's a school trip to the lunchbox museum, remember?" Nisha replied.

Evan shrugged. "I'm starving."

He asked nicely, and Mrs Butterworth gave him some more toast.

"I can't believe Doctor Bug got away," muttered Evan, as he dolloped strawberry jam on top.

"At least we saved the commissioner, her dogs, *and* the city," replied Nisha.

Evan was just about to take a bite of his toast when there was a loud munching sound.

"Hey, you did that without even moving your lips!" Nisha said with a laugh.

"That wasn't me," Evan replied, looking around. "It's coming from that wall."

"Wait! There's something outside," Nisha said, rushing to the window. "Look!"

Outside, hundreds of robot termites had surrounded the academy.

"It's a robotic army!" Evan yelled. "They're eating the walls!"

The whole building was being gobbled up by the tiny robots. Doctor Bug was hovering above them, gripping a remote control that he was using to direct the attack.

"I told you I'd be the number one villain!" he yelled into a tiny megaphone. "There's nothing more villainous than getting my termites to eat Hero Academy. Mwah-ha-ha-ha!"

Nisha and Evan looked at each other. This pesky villain was turning out to be rather annoying.

The Head appeared on a screen in the dinner hall, but the image kept breaking up. "I seem to have systems in my bugs ... I mean bugs in my system!" he cried, before the image disappeared completely.

Chapter 6:
In a jam

"We have to do something, or there'll be nothing left of the academy!" Evan said.

"I've got an idea," Nisha replied.

Once again, the two heroes spun into their super suits and raced outside.

Nimbus summoned up a gust of wind to try to blow the termites away, but there were too many of them.

"I'll go after Doctor Bug!" said Flex. He stretched his arms and tried to grab the tiny villain, but every time he got close, Doctor Bug just flew even higher out of reach. Before Flex knew what was happening, his arms were twisted into a knot.

"I'm stuck," Flex called out. "Completely stuck. Wait ... that's it – stuck! I've just had another idea, Nimbus."

"What do you mean?" asked Nimbus, desperately swatting away as many termites as she could.

"Nimbus, can you untangle my arms?" yelled Flex. "I need to get my toast."

"Now is not the time for snacking!" Nimbus shouted back.

"Trust me!" Flex said with a smile.

Nimbus summoned up another gust of wind to carry her into the air. Then she untangled Flex's arms.

"Thanks," said Flex, stretching his arm through the open window and grabbing the plate of toast and jam from the dinner hall.

Flex took a particularly jammy piece of toast and hurled it at Doctor Bug. The toast hit the villain and knocked him to the ground.

"Argh! I'm stuck!" Doctor Bug cried, trying to free himself from the jam. "Bleurgh. I hate strawberry jam!"

The more Doctor Bug wriggled and struggled, the more stuck he became. "Help me, robot termites!" he commanded.

His robot army didn't pay him any attention. Doctor Bug furiously jabbed the button on his controller, but nothing seemed to be happening.

"My controller won't work!" Doctor Bug wailed.

"Oh dear," Flex replied. "Is it *jammed*?"

Suddenly, the robot termites stopped in their tracks. They turned and began to scuttle away.

"Come back!" Doctor Bug commanded. "You must obey me. I'm the NUMBER ONE VILLAIN!"

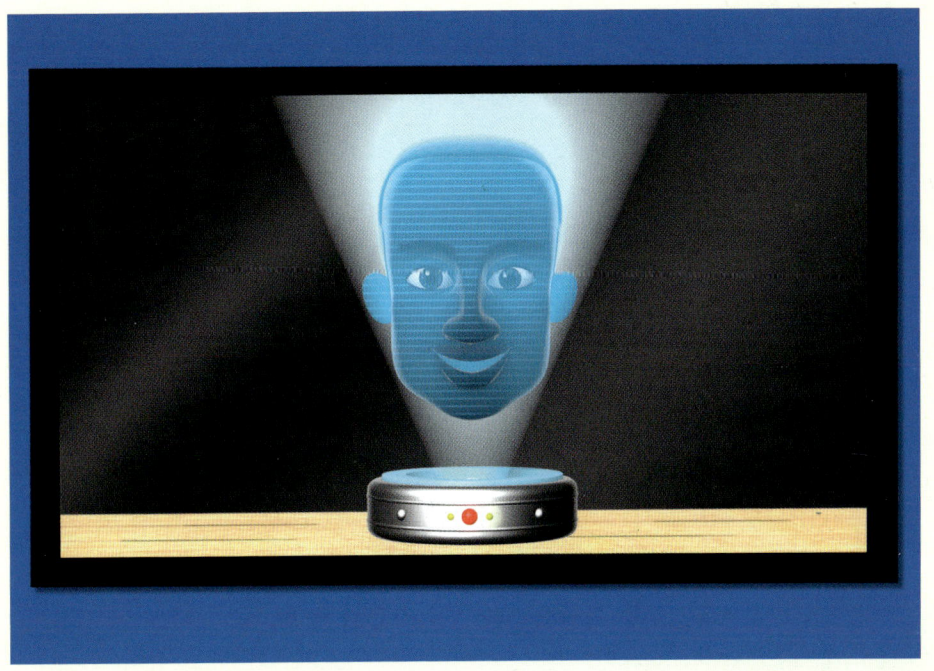

Soon enough, the whole of the robot army was scurrying away.

"Phew! We did it," Nimbus said. "What now?"

"Let's go and check on the Head," Flex said. He looked over at the tiny villain. "Doctor Bug isn't going anywhere!"

Inside, the Head appeared on the screen again. "Thank goodness. I'm much better now the bugs have gone," he said. "You two have saved the day ... again! Now let's make sure that Doctor Bug is locked away."

The next day, in Lexis City Jail …

"This picture is tiny. You can't even see my face!" Doctor Bug grumbled.

"Breakfast time!" a guard called out, opening the door.

"At least that's something to look forward to," Doctor Bug said. "What's on the menu?"

"Toast." The guard grinned. "I hope you like strawberry jam!"